PENG'S CHINESE TREASURY

Chinese Idioms

VOLUME 1

concept and cartoons
by
Tan Huay Peng

HEIAN

FIRST AMERICAN EDITION – 1987
Second Printing 1991

HEIAN INTERNATIONAL, INC.
P.O. Box 1013
Union City, CA 94587 USA.

First published in Singapore by
Times Books International
Times Centre, 1 New Industrial Road
Singapore 1953

ISBN 0-89346-289-6

Printed in Singapore

CONTENTS

LIST OF IDIOMS

INTRODUCTION

The impact of Chinese idioms

While having a conversation with a friend, scanning the newspapers, following the latest Chinese serials on television, or reading from a Chinese classic — in fact, in almost every situation — we are likely to stumble upon a Chinese idiom.

In the Chinese vocabulary, idioms are significant and integral vehicles of expression. Imagine how often we utter ever so glibly, the following: 手忙脚乱, 水落石出, 三心两意, 斤斤计较, 口是心非, or even 一刀两断! Then take an idiom like 马马虎虎, which literally means 'horses and tigers'. To the unenlightened, this would appear totally irrelevant. Where did these horses and tigers materialise from anyway? And to be sure, this is only an example of the many fascinating idioms in existence.

Proverb or idiom?

As there is much confusion concerning proverbs and idioms, it is best to make a distinction here. A proverb contains a definite message or philosophy of life, whereas an idiom has a wider application. It could either have a moral intent, or be an adept turn of phrase, a cogent expression with no deeper meaning. If an idiom delivers a wise thought or saying, it is in fact a proverb.

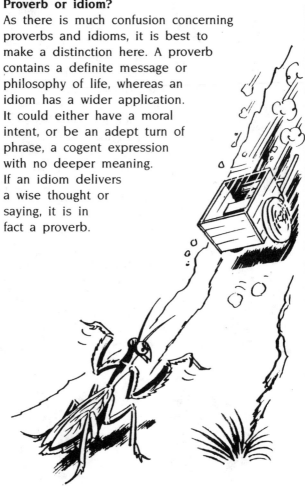

Types of idioms

There are those which are purely descriptive, like 风和日丽 or 古色古香. Some not only describe but seek to clarify and define more concisely. Sometimes they drive a point home by sheer exaggeration and emphasis. 垂涎三尺 and 对牛弹琴 are obvious examples.

A great number of Chinese idioms however allude to something deeper — many carry a moral or maxim, either directly or implicitly. Truly, it can be said that idioms reflect much of the wisdom and philosophy ingrained in Chinese culture.

Origins

Although idioms which have arisen from oral tradition and anonymous sources are many, quite a variety have their roots in literary origins, sayings of famous philosophers like Confucius and Mencius, or historical sources. All of these have grown into the heritage which we can richly draw upon.

志在四方

Idioms and their applications

What accounts for the popularity of idioms? First of all, relatively complex concepts may be fashioned into images everyone can relate to. Instead of declaring that one should not alert the enemy by engaging in impulsive actions, how much simpler to use the visual image created by 打草惊蛇, which clinches the meaning most effectively.

They inject colour and drama to speech and writing, and not just little ingots of wisdom but often much wit and subtle humour, as indeed the cartoons in this book will show. Idioms also have the advantage of economy of thought — the majority belong to the pithy, often rhythmic 4-character variety.

The approach of this book

There are a few thousand idioms being used perpetually in the Chinese language. The 125 explained and illustrated here, cartoon-fashion, are some of the most well-known and oft-heard, and applied easily to most familiar situations confronted in present-day society. Volume 2 deals with another 125 useful idioms.

The difficulty of understanding idioms sometimes lies in the inability to see the connection between the literal meaning and its underlying message. To solve this problem, literal translations are highlighted where appropriate, except in cases where the meaning is undisguised, as in 含辛茹苦 or 改过自新. Idioms with literary or historical origins are explained accordingly. There are also sentence examples to show usage.

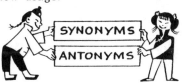

To encourage further reference, synonyms and antonyms, also idioms, are included wherever possible.

The two indexes which form the final section of the book are arranged alphabetically in Hanyu Pinyin and from classification of theme, providing a valuable checkpoint.

爱不释手　　ài bù shì shǒu

Meaning: To love something a great deal and not wish to part with it.

Example: 野菜布娃娃真有趣，每个有不同的特性和出生证书，怪不得孩子们都爱不释手。

按部就班   àn bù jiù bān

Literally: To follow a definite method or a prescribed procedure; keep to conventional ways of doing things.

Meaning: This is sometimes used derogatorily or critically to describe a bureaucratic, stick-in-the-mud attitude.

Example: 我们的教务主任时常教训我们做事要按部就班，不要乱七八糟。

Synonym: 循序渐进   xún xù jiàn jìn

Antonym: 别出心裁   bié chū xīn cái

百发百中 bǎi fā bǎi zhòng

Literally: A hundred shots, a hundred bull's eyes.

Meaning: Perfect marksmanship or unfailing accuracy. To be correct all the time.

Origin: Anecdotes of the Warring States. During the Spring and Autumn Period, King Gongwang of Chu had a follower named Yang Yongji who was an excellent archer. He established fame with his feat of repeatedly shooting through a willow leaf 100 paces away, hence the accolade of '百发百中'.

Example: 那气枪好手的枪法如神，百发百中。

Synonym: 百无一失　bǎi wú yī shī

百折不挠   bǎi zhé bù náo

Literally: To remain unshaken despite a hundred setbacks.

Meaning: Stoic behaviour in the face of all odds.

Example: 爱迪生凭着百折不挠的精神，在失败了许多次之后，终于发明了电灯。

Synonym: 坚韧不拔   jiān rèn bù bá

半途而废   bàn tú ér fèi

Literally: To abandon something halfway.

Meaning: Not see a thing through to its completion.

Origin: Luo Yang, who lived during the Warring States, left home to pursue his studies. After a year, he returned. His wife was then weaving cloth, but snipped the silken threads on her loom to show how efforts are wasted when one abandons things midway. Luo Yang persevered, eventually completing his studies 7 years later.

Example: 既然大家已费尽心机设计这部机器，就不要半途而废。

Antonym: 坚持不渝   jiān chí bù yú

包罗万象　　bāo luó wàn xiàng

Literally: To cover the myriad phenomena of the universe; things of all descriptions.

Meaning: All-inclusive and all-embracing.

Example: 美国国家图书馆的藏书丰富, 包罗万象, 古今中外的书本能在那儿找得到。

Synonym: 包含万有　bāo hán wàn yǒu

Antonym: 挂一漏万　guà yī lòu wàn

比比皆是 bǐ bǐ jiē shì

Literally: Here, there and everywhere.

Meaning: Can be found anywhere. Common.

Example: 泰国是个佛教盛行的国度，境内的寺庙比比皆是。

Synonym: 恒河沙数　héng hé shā shù

变本加厉   biàn běn jiā lì

Literally: To add to the severity of the original.

Meaning: Applies to a situation which worsens, or is aggravated or intensified.

Example: 他犯了大过被学校开除后，越发变本加厉，终日和一群不良少年混在一起胡闹。

标新立异　　biāo xīn lì yì

Literally: Exhibit/present something new to establish something different.

Meaning: Deliberately create something new to attract attention. Favourable as well as unfavourable in meaning, depending on the context.

Example: 彩装少年在服装上标新立异，无非是想引起别人的注意吧了。

别出心裁　bié chū xīn cái

Literally: To adopt a new style.

Meaning: A fresh approach or method — said of a pioneering, enterprising spirit.

Example: 编剧者的构思巧妙，别出心裁，不用布景而仰赖演员的动作表现出"时"与"地"，打破了舞台演出的局限。

Synonym: 别开生面　bié kāi shēng miàn

Antonym: 依样画葫芦　yī yàng huà hú lú

不打自招   bù dǎ zì zhāo

Literally: To confess without having to be beaten.

Meaning: To give oneself away; to reveal one's bad intentions unwittingly, without any external pressure or coercion.

Example: 辨方证人在控方律师的巧妙问话下，不打自招，泄露了曾受贿于被告的事实。

不攻自破　　　　bù gōng zì pò

Literally: Breaks by itself even without being attacked.

Meaning: Explains that there is no logic or foundation involved (e.g. in an argument, a rumour or an allegation).

Example: 在事实面前，谣言必然不攻自破。

不堪设想　　bù kān shè xiǎng

Meaning: Suggests that the consequences would be too dreadful or unspeakable to contemplate.

Example: 幸亏司机刹车刹得快，不然后果不堪设想。

不可救药   bù kě jiù yào

Literally: (An illness) which medicine would be unable to cure.

Meaning: Beyond remedy. Incorrigible. Applied to a situation which is hopelessly bad.

Example: 他犯罪多次，真是到了不可救药的地步了。

不可思议　　bù kě sī yì

Literally: Inconceivable; unimaginable.

Meaning: Difficult to fathom; anything having an element of mystery.

Origin: Derived from Buddhist teachings. This intimated that there were regions which the human mind could not grasp. The idiom has since become secular in usage.

Example: 新加坡的一层七层楼酒店，竟然会在转眼间倒塌下来，真是不可思议。

Synonym: 莫测高深　　mò cè gāo shēn

Antonym: 尽在意中　　jìn zài yì zhōng

不劳而获 bù láo ér huò

Literally: Enjoy the fruits of the harvest without having to work for it.

Meaning: Obtain results without putting in any effort. Describes a lazy person's way of doing things.

Example: 成功是靠勤勉努力得来的，世上哪有不劳而获的道理?

Antonym: 徒劳无功 tú láo wú gōng

不偏不倚　　　bù piān bù yǐ

Literally: Neither leaning to one side nor the other.

Meaning: Being perfectly impartial, neutral and objective.

Example: 陪审团是应该对每个案件有公正的判决，不偏不倚。

Synonym: 铁面无私　　tiě miàn wú sī

不胜枚举   bù shèng méi jǔ

Literally: Not possible to single out every one.

Meaning: Too many to mention; a countless number.

Example: 台湾有"蝴蝶王国"之称，所产的蝴蝶，种类繁多，不胜枚举。

不闻不问 bù wén bù wèn

Literally: Neither listening nor asking.

Meaning: To be totally indifferent; not in the least concerned or curious about anything.

Example: 许多本地学生对世界大事不闻不问，毫不关心。

不务正业　　bù wù zhèng yè

Literally: Not attending to things which are relevant to one's own occupation.

Meaning: Used in describing unemployed vagrants or tramps, or those who persist in dabbling in affairs outside of their proper occupations.

Example: 一个人如果整天闲荡，不务正业，一定不会有出息。

Synonym: 游手好闲　 yóu shǒu hào xián

不省人事　　bù xǐng rén shì

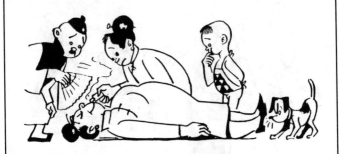

Literally: Not aware of human affairs.

Meaning: Lose consciousness, from illness or shock, or in an accident.

Example: 美珍参加全国马拉松赛跑，跑完了最后一圈再也支持不住，"叭"的一声倒下，不省人事。

不言而喻　　　bù yán ér yù

Literally: Can be understood although nothing has been said or explained.

Meaning: Self-evident. Can be easily deduced from the circumstances one is confronted with.

Example: 旅馆服务生把行李送进客房后，仍旧挨挨蹭蹭不离去，不言而喻，是希望我们给点小费。

不遗余力　　　　bù yí yú lì

Literally: No strength or energy left over.

Meaning: To put all one's efforts into a task or job. Total dedication.

Example: 他是个华乐爱好者，对于推广华乐向来不遗余力。

Synonym: 全力以赴　quán lì yǐ fù

不翼而飞 bù yì ér fēi

Literally: Having no wings, yet flying away.

Meaning: Disappearing without a trace, vanishing mysteriously. The idiom also refers to the rapid spreading of news or information.

Example: 我原本放在抽屉里的一笔钱不翼而飞，到底是谁拿了？

Synonym: 不胫而走　bù jìng ér zǒu

不约而同   bù yuē ér tóng

Meaning: Acting in accord without prior consultation. Often used to describe a surprising coincidence.

Example: 说来也真巧，在新年的前一天，同事们都不约而同地穿了新衣来上班。

Synonym: 不谋而合   bù móu ér hé

Antonym: 同床异梦   tóng chuáng yì mèng

不择手段   bù zé shǒu duàn

Literally: Not selective about the method used.

Meaning: Applies especially to an unscrupulous person, who stops at nothing to attain his goal — whether or not fair or foul means are applied.

Example: 有的人为了本身的利益，会不择手段地去打击别人。

不自量力 bù zì liàng lì

Meaning: Overrate one's own abilities; not taking a proper measure of one's strength. A similar idiom brings the meaning out most vividly, and this is naturally the well-known one of the praying mantis trying to stop a cart!

Example: 小国竟然敢跟大国对抗，不免被讥为不自量力。

Synonym: 螳臂当车　táng bì dāng chē

长年累月　　cháng nián lěi yuè

Literally: For many years, and months on end.

Meaning: This is to express a long duration of time.

Example: 经过长年累月的学习，杰克终于把修理汽车这门技术学上手了。

Synonym: 经年累月　jīng nián lěi yuè

趁火打劫 *chèn huǒ dǎ jié*

Literally: To rob and plunder during a fire.

Meaning: To take advantage of an unfortunate circumstance; profiting from a time of confusion and chaos.

Example: 放高利贷者看准别人等钱急用，就放债生息，从中取利。这无疑是趁火打劫的行为。

Synonym: 混水摸鱼　hùn shuǐ mō yú

愁眉不展　　chóu méi bù zhǎn

Literally: Knitted or furrowed brows.

Meaning: Aptly describes a person who is burdened with worry and anxiety, as if the weight of the world is upon his shoulders. Gloomy and downcast.

Example: 他整天愁眉不展，不知道是为财政上的难题而烦恼呢？

Synonym: 垂头丧气　　chuí tóu sàng qì

Antonym: 笑逐颜开　　xiào zhú yán kāi

川流不息　　chuān liú bù xī

Literally: To flow continuously.

Meaning: Any uninterrupted flow of persons, vehicles or ships. A descriptive idiom which describes the flow of human or vehicular traffic.

Example: 傍晚的王府井大街上，行人和自行车川流不息，好不热闹。

Synonym: 络绎不绝　　luò yì bù jué

吹毛求疵　　chuī máo qiú cī

Literally: To blow the hair aside expecting to find a blemish or defect.

Meaning: To find fault deliberately. Nitpicking.

Example: 做生意的人要生意兴隆，得有好脾气；尽管顾客吹毛求疵，也不能生气。

垂涎三尺　　chuí xián sān chǐ

Literally: Drooling with as much as 3 feet of saliva.

Meaning: Describes the look of an extremely greedy or covetous person, or someone consumed with desire.

Example: 小贩中心里售卖的食品众多，有引人垂涎三尺的烤鸡，烧鸭，有消暑解渴的大西瓜和冷冻甜品。

唇亡齿寒　　chún wáng chǐ hán

Literally: If the lips are gone, the teeth will feel cold.

Meaning: A condition of mutual dependence.

Origin: Zuo Qinming's Chronicles.
This is the story of the 2 small related states of Guo and Yu. The ruler of Jin, wanting to attack Guo, had to pass through Yu first, and bribed the King of Yu with jade and horses. But alas! As soon as Guo fell under the Jin army, Yu's vulnerability was exposed, and it was the next to be conquered.

Example: 正所谓唇亡齿寒，邻国如果落入敌人手中，我国也难以保全。

从容不迫　　ōng róng bù pò

Meaning: In a calm and unhurried manner. Take things in one's stride.

Example: 大家请老校长致词，他从容不迫地站起来说了一番感人的话。

Antonym: 手忙脚乱　shǒu máng jiǎo luàn

措手不及　　cuò shǒu bù jí

Literally: Not in time to deal with (something), (a situation).

Meaning: To be caught off guard; to be unprepared.

Example: 对方球员起板扣杀，我一时措手不及，误球失分。

打草惊蛇   **dǎ cǎo jīng shé**

Literally: Beat the grass and scare off the snakes.

Meaning: To alert the enemy (or others) by one's impulsive actions.

Origin: Anecdotes of the Kaiyuan and Tianbao Reigns. Wang Lu was a corrupt magistrate of the Tang Dynasty. One day, he came across a complaint against a subordinate, which implicated himself. Marvelling at his narrow escape, he wrote: 'You may only have beaten the grass, but I've been frightened like the snake hiding in it.'

Example: 警方在采取扫荡行动之前，极力保持隐密，以免打草惊蛇。

Antonym: 不动声色   bù dòng shēng sè

大刀阔斧 dà dāo kuò fǔ

Literally: A large knife and a broad axe.

Meaning: Bold and resolute action. To settle a matter decisively with no shilly-shallying. To take a decisive step.

Example: 公司的新经理一上任，就进行大刀阔斧的改革。

Antonym: 优柔寡断　yōu róu guǎ duàn

大公无私　　dà gōng wú sī

Meaning:　Entirely objective, with no selfish interests (or individual desires).

Origin:　During the Spring and Autumn Period, Duke Pinggong of Jin asked Qi Huangyang, 'Nanyang County needs a magistrate. Can you recommend anyone?' Much to his surprise, Qi suggested his enemy Xie Hu. Later, the Duke said a new judge was needed in the imperial court. And this time, Qi suggested his own son. Confucius learnt of this and commended Qi highly for his selflessness — neither prejudiced nor afraid of gossip.

Example:　在上位的人大公无私，赏罚分明，才能使下属信服。

大同小异   dà tóng xiǎo yì

Meaning: Generally similar except for slight differences.

Example: 你们俩的作文大同小异，到底是谁抄谁的？

大言不惭　　dà yán bù cán

Meaning: Unabashed. Used to describe a person who is fond of boasting and bragging.

Example: 这家伙最会吹牛，说自己是个艺术天才，大言不惭说个不停，真叫人讨厌。

当机立断　　dāng jī lì duàn

Meaning: To make a decision when an opportunity presents itself.

Example: 趁着股价上涨，你应该当机立断，把股票脱手。

Antonym: 举棋不定　jǔ qí bù dìng

当仁不让　　dāng rén bù ràng

Meaning: To bear the responsibility and not shirk from it.

Example: 在这次的救灾行动中, 小妹也当仁不让, 捐出了扑满。

道听途说   dào tīng tú shuō

Literally: What is heard on the road is reported to others.

Meaning: Hearsay; gossip. Unfounded rumours.

Example: 李大嫂的消息，都是道听途说而来，千万不可相信。

Synonym: 街谈巷议   jiē tán xiàng yì

Antonym: 真凭实据   zhēn píng shí jù

得不偿失   dé bù cháng shī

Meaning: The loss far outweighs the gain. Gain is insignificant compared to the heavy losses incurred.

Example: 许多人把辛苦省下的钱买彩票和万字票，希望能发一笔横财，结果却是得不偿失，所下的赌注远超过所赢取的奖金。

得寸进尺　　dé cùn jìn chǐ

Literally: Demanding a foot after gaining an inch.

Meaning: Insatiable greed; never satisfied.

Example: 隔壁的李嫂向来借了东西不还，最近她得寸进尺，竟然开口借钱。

Synonym: 得陇望蜀　dé lǒng wàng shǔ

Antonym: 心满意足　xīn mǎn yì zú

得过且过　　dé guò qiě guò

Meaning: To get by, or muddle along. An attitude of complacency.

Origin: According to legend, there was a bird called Hanhao that lived in the Wutai Mountains. In the summertime it was endowed with colourful feathers. But soon it was winter, and the lovely feathers vanished. As the bird shivered in the cold, it cried out, 'Muddling along! Muddling along!' All to be forgotten when summer came around again.

Example: 我们活着得有目标和理想，断不能抱着得过且过的态度过日子。

Synonym: 马马虎虎　　mǎ mǎ hū hū

Antonym: 精益求精　　jīng yì qiú jīng

得意忘形　　dé yì wàng xíng

Meaning: So overjoyed and delighted that one is not in total control of one's senses.

Example: 眼看所支持的足球队又进了一球，老郭得意忘形之下，猛拍旁人的肩膀。

Antonym: 心灰意懒　xīn huī yì lǎn

对牛弹琴   duì niú tán qín

Literally: Playing the lute to a cow.

Meaning: This suggests the futility of explaining to people who cannot understand, either because they are stupid or have no interest in the subject, or because it is out of their depth.

Origin: The Hongming Encyclopaedia of Buddhism. The musician Gongming Yi was playing his lute when he saw a cow munching grass nearby. To attract its attention, he started producing sounds like the buzzing of mosquitoes and the mooing of a calf.

Example: 讲师的授课对我来说简直是对牛弹琴，因为我完全抓不住它的意思。

对症下药 　duì zhèng xià yào

Literally: To apply medicine best suited to the illness.

Meaning: Understand the problem before trying to solve it.

Origin: History of the Three Kingdoms. Hua Tuo was a famous physician who lived at the end of the Han Dynasty. Once 2 prefectural officials Ni Xun and Li Yan came to see him complaining of headache and fever. He prescribed different medicines for them. His explanation was that Ni Xun's ailment was indigestion and Li Yan's a cold.

Example: 产品滞销的原因不一，唯有对症下药，想出解决的办法，才能打开销路。

发扬光大 fā yáng guāng dà

Literally: To carry forward and brighten.

Meaning: To develop and enhance — in other words, to give a glorious appearance to something.

Example: 传统戏曲的发扬光大，全落在年轻一辈人的身上。

反复无常　　fǎn fù wú cháng

Meaning: To be always fickle (in thought and behaviour). Not consistent.

Example: 林姑娘的脾气反复无常，一会儿高兴，一会儿生气，叫追求她的小伙子摸不准。

Antonym: 始终不渝　shǐ zhōng bù yú

废寝忘食 fèi qǐn wàng shí

Literally: Forget about food and sleep.

Meaning: Frequently used to describe a person who is so determined to accomplish his goal that he brushes everything aside. Also, total concentration on task at hand.

Example: 下星期就是会考了，学生们废寝忘食努力地温习功课。

Synonym: 发愤忘食 fā fèn wàng shí

奋不顾身　fèn bù gù shēn

Meaning: To be so dauntless as to be unconcerned about one's own safety. A self-sacrificial attitude.

Example: 阿里奋不顾身救人的行为，受到了当局的表扬。

Antonym: 贪生怕死　tān shēng pà sǐ

风驰电掣   fēng chí diàn chè

Literally: As swift as the wind and a flash of lightning.

Meaning: Breathtaking speed.

Example: 摩托船载满了乘客，风驰电掣般向着邦咯岛驶去。

风和日丽 fēng hé rì lì

Literally: Bright sun and gentle breeze.

Meaning: Fine climatic conditions – sunny and breezy. Fair weather.

Example: 这一天风和日丽，万里无云，正是郊游的好天气。

奉公守法　fèng gōng shǒu fǎ

Meaning: Observe rules and regulations. Be law-abiding.

Example: 他一向奉公守法，绝不会干出犯法的事来。

Antonym: 胡作非为　hú zuò fēi wéi

敷衍塞责　　fū yǎn sè zé

Meaning: Carrying out responsibilities in a perfunctory fashion.

Example: 你的工作态度敷衍塞责，又怎会获得提升？

Synonym: 得过且过　　dé guò qiě guò

Antonym: 一丝不苟　　yī sī bù gǒu

改过自新　　　gǎi guò zì xīn

Meaning: To correct one's errors and make a fresh start. The English idiomatic equivalent is to mend one's ways or to turn over a new leaf.

Example: 他经过这次的教训后，下定决心改过自新。

Synonyms: 痛改前非　tòng gǎi qián fēi
洗心革面　xǐ xīn gé miàn

Antonym: 变本加厉　biàn běn jiā lì

高枕无忧　　gāo zhěn wú yōu

Literally: Prop up the pillow and have no worries.

Meaning: Referring to an absolutely carefree and relaxed existence, especially after certain obstacles or difficulties have already been overcome.

Example: 国内的异端分子，已被驱逐出境，独裁统治者以为可以高枕无忧了。

Synonym: 高枕而卧　gāo zhěn ér wò

隔岸观火　　　gé àn guān huǒ

Literally: Watch a fire from across the river.

Meaning: Aware of others' difficulties and problems, yet making no attempt to help or get involved. To remain indifferent.

Example: 众人隔岸观火，欣赏这一出"夫妻吵架"的好戏上演。

Synonym: 袖手旁观　　xiù shǒu páng guān

格格不入　　　gé gé bù rù

Literally: So square that it will not fit.

Meaning: Be incompatible with, a misfit. The English equivalent: a square peg in a round hole.

Example: 感情是不能够勉强的，既然我们的性情格格不入，继续来往是没有什么好结果。

Synonym: 方枘圆凿　fāng ruì yuán zuò

Antonym: 水乳交融　shuǐ rǔ jiāo róng

各有千秋　　gè yǒu qiān qiū

Literally: Each has a thousand autumns.

Meaning: Each has its enduring qualities or merits.

Example: 中国和日本女排的球艺各有千秋。比赛结果，双方打成了平手。

根深蒂固　　gēn shēn dì gù

Literally: Deep-rooted and as firmly attached as the fruit is to the stalk.

Meaning: Firmly established. This could refer to a belief, a trait, or a habit.

Example: 重男轻女的观念还是根深蒂固地存在老一辈的思想中。

供不应求   gōng bù yìng qiú

Meaning: The supply is insufficient to meet demand.

Example: 这本语文辞典一面市，即供不应求，被人们抢购一空。

钩心斗角 gōu xīn dòu jiǎo

Literally: To hook the heart and fight with horns.

Meaning: To conspire, scheme against each other.

Origin: This started out as a description of the intricate structures within a palace, of the many corridors, courtyards, inner chambers, etc.

Example: 为了争夺高位,他们俩暗地里勾心斗角。

Synonym: 明争暗斗 míng zhēng àn dòu

孤陋寡闻　　gū lòu guǎ wén

Literally: Isolated, rustic and deprived of news.

Meaning: Unknowledgeable, uninformed;
descriptive of a cloistered attitude.

Example: 想不到你连孔子也没听说过，真是孤陋
寡闻得可以。

Synonyms: 井底之蛙　jǐng dǐ zhī wā
坐井观天　zuò jǐng guān tiān

孤掌难鸣　gū zhǎng nán míng

Literally: It is difficult to produce sound with one palm.

Meaning: It is difficult to achieve anything singlehandedly, or depending on one person's strength alone. Rather, a pooling of resources and efforts is more likely to produce the desired results.

Example: 其他人在会议上都支持科长的主张，小王虽不同意，但孤掌难鸣，不便发言。

Synonyms: 独木不成林　dú mù bù chéng lín
独木难支　　dú mù nán zhī

Antonym: 众志成城　　zhòng zhì chéng chéng

古色古香　　gǔ sè gǔ xiāng

Literally: Old in colour and fragrance.

Meaning: Antiquated and quaint. Mainly descriptive of curios, furniture, or of general atmosphere.

Example: 会堂大厅的布置古色古香，充满了典雅的气氛。

拐弯抹角　guǎi wān mò jiǎo

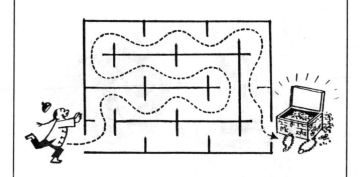

Literally: Turn bends and go round corners.

Meaning: Do or say things in a roundabout fashion instead of going straight to the point.

Example: 不要再拐弯抹角了，担白说出你的意思吧!

Antonyms: 开门见山　kāi mén jiàn shān
单刀直入　dān dāo zhí rù

光明正大　guāng míng zhèng dà

Meaning: Honest and upright. Commonly used idiom to declare the righteousness of one's actions. Not shifty or having suspicious motives.

Example: 就胜负两方来说，赢要赢得光明正大，输要输得光荣。

Synonym: 光明磊落　guāng míng lěi luò

Antonym: 鬼鬼祟祟　guǐ guǐ suì suì

含辛茹苦　　hán xīn rú kǔ

Meaning: Endure suffering and hardship. Used especially to describe lives fraught with difficulties and struggles.

Example: 谢大妈含辛茹苦地把儿子抚养成人，儿子却不孝顺她。

好高骛远　hào gāo wù yuǎn

Literally: To like and pursue height and distance.

Meaning: To strive for or hanker after the unattainable, and whatever lies beyond one's grasp. Having unrealistic dreams.

Example: 小罗为人好高骛远，不求实际，不是理想的结婚对象。

Antonym: 脚踏实地　jiǎo tà shí dì

好逸恶劳　　　hào yì wù láo

Literally: Love ease and hate work.

Meaning: Typical characteristics of a loafer.

Example: 好逸恶劳是目前年轻人的一般通病。

和睦相处 hé mù xiāng chǔ

Meaning: Living in harmony.

Example: 邻居们若能彼此容忍，关心，就能和睦相处，省却许多不必要的争执。

横冲直撞 héng chōng zhí zhuàng

Meaning: Pushing through by shoving and elbowing one's way. These strong-arm tactics can in fact be taken either literally or metaphorically.

Example: 汤米开车向来横冲直撞，不遵守交通规则，难怪会发生车祸!

狐假虎威 hú jiǎ hǔ wēi

Literally: Fox borrows from the tiger's might.

Meaning: Relying on another's power and strength to dominate and bully others.

Origin: Anecdotes of the Warring States. This is a famous fable of the crafty fox who, wishing to prove that he was the King of the Forest, stalked through the forest in front of the tiger. Naturally all the animals, seeing the tiger, were terrified and scurried off at once.

Example: 越南狐假虎威，悍然发动白柬之战，行径令人发指。

胡思乱想　　hú sī luàn xiǎng

Meaning: To engage in wild thoughts; to let the imagination run wild.

Example: 深夜回家，走在冷清清的街道上，我不由得胡思乱想起来。

胡作非为　　hú zuò fēi wéi

Meaning: Act in defiance of the law or public opinion. To commit all kinds of outrage.

Example: 张管工在厂中胡作非为，工人们都痛恨他。

花言巧语 huā yán qiǎo yǔ

Literally: Flowery and deceitful speech.

Meaning: Flattery, words of insincerity spoken to beguile and deceive.

Example: 在骗子的花言巧语下，何嫂买下了一块据说有治疗疾病功效的"神石"。

Synonym: 甜言密语　tián yán mì yǔ

画蛇添足　　huà shé tiān zú

Literally: Draw a snake and then add feet to it.

Meaning: Do more than is necessary, thus ruining what would otherwise have been perfect.

Origin: Anecdotes of the Warring States. A family in the state of Chu had one pot of wine to be shared among its stewards, so it was suggested that the first to draw a snake could drink the wine. The first man to finish decided to add in the feet. However, as snakes have no feet, his drink was forfeited!

Example: 小说的结尾带出了一大段的议论以点明主题，这未免有画蛇添足之嫌。

挥金如土　huī jīn rú tǔ

Literally: Throw money about like dirt.

Meaning: Squander money; to be spendthrift, careless with money.

Example: 在一些国家里，穷人的三餐成问题，富人却过着夜夜笙歌，挥金如土的生活。

Antonym: 一毛不拔　yī máo bù bá

混水摸鱼 hún shuǐ mō yú

Literally: To grope for fish in muddy waters.

Meaning: Taking advantage of and gaining from a time of turmoil and general chaos.

Example: 在纽约全市电流中断的那个晚上，罪案频频发生，还有人混水摸鱼,抢掠商店。

Synonym: 趁火打劫　chèn huǒ dǎ jié

鸡犬不宁　　jī quǎn bù níng

Literally: Chickens and dogs are not at peace.

Meaning: Great disorder and chaos prevails.

Example: 隔壁人家通宵开舞会，吵得左邻右舍鸡犬不宁。

Antonym: 鸡犬无惊　jī quǎn wú jīng

家喻户晓　　jiā yù hù xiǎo

Literally: Known to every household.

Meaning: Known to everyone; widely known.

Example: 嫦娥奔月是一个家喻户晓的故事。

Synonym: 家传户诵　jiā chuán hù sòng

驾轻就熟　　*jià qīng jiù shú*

Literally: Drive a light carriage on a familiar road.

Meaning: Performing a task with ease because of previous experience and familiarity.

Example: 黄小姐在会计部工作了多年，对于有关工作早已驾轻就熟，调任为主任相信是胜任有余的。

见异思迁 jiàn yì sī qiān

Literally: Clamouring for a change when something new is seen.

Meaning: Fickle, capricious; changeable.

Example: 大华见一个爱一个，见异思迁，十分不可靠。

见义勇为　　jiàn yì yǒng wéi

Meaning: Be unafraid of doing whatever is just and righteous. This describes an honourable and commendable attitude.

Example: 这几位青年见义勇为，合力制服盗贼的行为确实值得嘉奖。

捷足先登　　jié zú xiān dēng

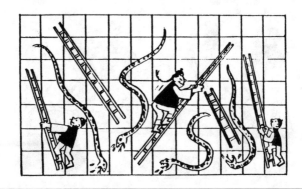

Literally: The swift-footed will be the first to reach the top.

Meaning: If you wish to succeed, be quick about it, otherwise others will get there before you.

Example: 听说音乐会的门票难买，还好我捷足先登，买到了两张门票。

近朱者赤，近墨者黑
jìn zhū zhě chì, jìn mò zhě hēi

Literally: If one is near vermilion, one becomes red; if one is near ink, one becomes black.

Meaning: A vivid way of describing the importance of one's environment, and the likelihood of being influenced by the company one keeps.

Example: 近朱者赤，近墨者黑，这俗语讲得真有道理，谨慎选择朋友是必要的。

Synonym: 染於仓则仓, rǎn yú cāng zé cāng,
染於黄则黄 rǎn yú huáng zé huáng

井井有条　　jǐng jǐng yǒu tiáo

Meaning: Everything in its proper place; in a perfectly orderly manner.

Example: 职业妇女身兼两职，既工作，又理家，但只要有计划，还是能把家务打理得井井有条的。

Synonym: 有条不紊　　yǒu tiáo bù wèn

Antonym: 杂乱无章　　zá luàn wú zhāng

刻苦耐劳   kè kǔ nài láo

Meaning: To endure suffering and hardship.

Example: 四姨丈的食品公司有今天的成就全靠他
二十年来刻苦耐劳所获的。

Synonym: 吃苦耐劳   chī kǔ nài láo

路不拾遗 lù bù shí yí

Literally: No one picks up what's left by the wayside.

Meaning: Honesty prevails throughout society. To describe a society with high moral standards.

Example: 生活在理想的"乌托邦"是很幸福的，路不拾遗，丰衣足食。

Synonym: 夜不闭户　　yè bù bì hù

落花流水 　　luò huā liú shuǐ

Literally: Like fallen flowers carried away by flowing water.

Meaning: An idiom which describes failure or defeat, or a sorry plight. Used particularly in circumstances of battle or war, when one side has been completely vanquished.

Example: 我方的军队把敌人打得落花流水，大败逃走。

慢条斯理 màn tiáo sī lǐ

Meaning: Slowly and unhurriedly. Going about one's affairs in a leisurely manner.

Example: 乘客们都急切地等着办理签证手续，机场人员却慢条斯理地执行任务。

普天同庆　　　pǔ tiān tóng qìng

Literally: The whole world joins in celebration.

Meaning: Universal joy.

Example: 圣诞节是全世界各地普天同庆的佳日。

千变万化　qiān biàn wàn huà

Literally: A thousand changes and ten thousand variations.

Meaning: Ever-changing, never the same. Dynamic.

Example: 关岛的天气，几乎天天一样；云却千变万化，每日不同。

倾盆大雨   qīng pén dà yǔ

Meaning: Heavy downpour; torrential rain.

Example: 中午下的一场倾盆大雨, 使到路面浸水, 车辆无法通行。

情同手足　　qíng tóng shǒu zú

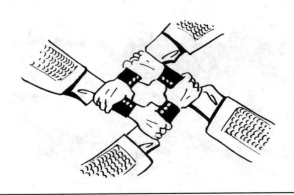

Literally: As intimately connected as limbs to the body.

Meaning: To have a close brotherly relationship.

Example: 他们虽然不是同胞兄弟，可是在困难的时候，却能情同手足互相照顾。

荣华富贵　　róng huá fù guì

Meaning: Possessing glory, wealth and honour.

Example: 荣华富贵是许多人追求的目标；追求不到，就怨自己的命运不好。

三五成群　　　sān wǔ chéng qún

Literally: In groups or clusters of threes and fives.

Meaning: Wherever people are gathered together in small groups — and these can be bystanders, friends, students, etc. — this idiom can be used.

Example: 跳楼事件发生后，路人三五成群地聚在一起议论。

视死如归　　shì sǐ rú guī

视死如归

Literally: To regard death as returning home.

Meaning: Courage and fortitude even when confronted with death or disaster. An admirable attitude.

Example: 我方的兵士视死如归，勇猛作战，在战事上取得极大的胜利。

Antonym: 贪生怕死　tān shēng pà sǐ

手舞足蹈   shǒu wǔ zú dǎo

Literally: Dancing about energetically, with hands and legs in perpetual motion.

Meaning: An expression of joy and exhilaration.

Example: 弟弟听到有马戏可看，高兴得手舞足蹈起来。

守望相助　shǒu wàng xiāng zhù

Meaning: To watch over and help one another.
Provide mutual help and protection.
Used to describe the ideal neighbourly
attitude.

Example: "守望相助"计划实行后，组屋内的犯罪
案件果然大为减少。

四通八达 sì tōng bā dá

Literally: Four thoroughfares and eight destinations.

Meaning: To describe accessibility and good communication. Accessible from all sides.

Example: 上海是中国的第一大商业城市，交通四通八达，非常方便。

为非作歹 wéi fēi zuò dǎi

Meaning: To make mischief and evil; to commit misdeeds.

Example: 为非作歹的匪徒终于被警方拘捕，真是大快人心。

Antonym: 奉公守法　fèng gōng shǒu fǎ

无微不至   wú wēi bù zhì

Literally: To take care of every minute detail; to be meticulous.

Meaning: This is an idiom which describes painstaking care and concern, like that of a parent for a child, or even of a doctor or nurse for a patient.

Example: 在我生病期间, 母亲无微不至地照顾我, 自己却累倒了。

相安无事　　xiāng ān wú shì

Meaning: To live in peace without disputes or conflicts; to live together harmoniously.

Example: 林家与陈家比邻而居，向来相安无事，没想到最近却因一点小事而争吵起来。

Synonym: 和睦相处　hé mù xiāng chǔ

兴高采烈　　　xìng gāo cǎi liè

Meaning: To be in high spirits; to be exuberant.

Example: 我们班上的同学得到全校最好的成绩，
大家兴高采烈地庆祝。

Synonym: 眉飞色舞　méi fēi sè wǔ

Antonyms: 愁眉苦脸　chóu méi kǔ liǎn
闷闷不乐　mèn mèn bù lè

袖手旁观　xiù shǒu páng guān

Literally: To stand aside and observe, hands folded in sleeves.

Meaning: To remain indifferent and uninvolved, the implication here being that though others may be in a quandary, no attempt is made to render help.

Example: 一般行人对路上遇到交通意外的事件却袖手旁观。

Synonym: 隔岸观火　gé àn guān huǒ

Antonym: 自告奋勇　zì gào fèn yǒng

鸦雀无声　　yā què wú shēng

Literally: Not a sound from crows and sparrows.

Meaning: Deathly silent; extremely quiet.

Example: 会场上鸦雀无声，只有独唱者的歌声在空中飘荡。

Antonym: 人声鼎沸　rén shēng dǐng fèi

一落千丈　yī luò qiān zhàng

Literally: To drop 3000 metres.

Meaning: Used in describing a sharp decline, or a drastic decline.

Example: 由于受到经济不景气的影响，父亲的生意一落千丈。

Antonym: 扶摇直上　fú yáo zhí shàng

一模一样　　yī mó yī yàng

Meaning: Exactly the same. Or, to use an English equivalent, like two peas in a pod.

Example: 这对双生兄弟长得一模一样，叫人难以分辨。

一事无成　yī shì wú chéng

Meaning: To have nothing accomplished.

Example: 有些人在失败后不知反省，不求改进，结果当然是一事无成。

一无所有

yī wú suǒ yǒu

Meaning: To have nothing at all; to have no possessions. A condition of poverty or destitution.

Example: 一场大火夺去了我的身家财产，我已变得一无所有了。

一知半解   yī zhī bàn jiě

Meaning: Having only a partial understanding of something.

Example: 读书须求彻底明了，一知半解或不求甚解都不是读书应有的态度。

以身作则　　　yǐ shēn zuò zé

Meaning: To set a good example.

Example: 言教不如身教，“以身作则”往往能收到良好的效果。

饮水思源　yǐn shuǐ sī yuán

Literally: When you drink water, consider its source.

Meaning: Always bear in mind how the past has contributed to one's present situation.

Origin: Yu Xin (513–581), a man of letters, was sent to the Western Wei Dynasty as an envoy of the Liang Dynasty. Later he became a prominent official in the Western Wei court. But Yu Xin never forgot his old homeland, and wrote this poem in appreciation: 'When you eat fruit, think of the tree that bore it. When you drink water, think of its source.'

Example: 我们生活在这美丽的土地上，饮水思源，不能不感激辛勤开荒的先辈们。

雨过天晴　　yǔ guò tiān qíng

Literally: The sun shines again after the rain.

Meaning: Indicating a favourable change in climate or circumstance.

Example: 亚明被人所害，经过一年的打官司，才洗脱罪名，全家人正如雨过天晴，皆大欢喜。

与日俱增　yǔ rì jù zēng

Meaning: To increase with each passing day; often applies to the strengthening or deepening of a relationship.

Example: 这些年来，他们的感情与日俱增，成为知心的朋友。

争先恐后 zhēng xiān kǒng hòu

Literally: Striving always to be the first, fearing to lag behind.

Meaning: Certainly apt in describing man's competitive spirit in everything he does, and his urge to get ahead of everybody else.

Origin: The Book of Han Fei Zi

Example: 大家排队守秩序，就可避免争先恐后，强者抢先，弱者居后的现象。

蒸蒸日上　zhēng zhēng rì shàng

Literally: Water evaporates into steam.

Meaning: This describes steady growth and rapid progress, referring mainly to the economy or in areas of work.

Example: 自从改变营业方针后，公司的业务蒸蒸日上，营业额远超过去年。

Synonym: 扶摇直上　fú yáo zhí shàng

Antonym: 每况愈下　měi kuàng yù xià

志同道合　　zhì tóng dào hé

Meaning: To be motivated by the same principles; to cherish the same ideal and follow the same path. Unity of purpose.

Example: 在人生的道路上，若能找到志同道合的朋友，那就死而无憾了。

Antonym: 背道而驰　bèi dào ér chí

置之不理　　　zhì zhī bù lǐ

Meaning: To disregard entirely; to ignore and set aside. To treat with indifference.

Example: 现代的年青人如不听父母的勤告，置之不理，将来一定会后悔的。

Synonym: 置之脑后　　zhì zhī nǎo hòu

装聋作哑 zhuāng lóng zuò yǎ

Literally: Pretending to be deaf and dumb.

Meaning: To feign ignorance. To pretend that one is unaware of what is going on.

Example: 难道你以为装聋作哑，就可以避免回答我的问题吗？

Synonym: 充耳不闻 chōng ér bù wén

Antonym: 洗耳恭听 xǐ ěr gōng tīng

HANYU PINYIN INDEX

CLASSIFIED INDEX

CHINESE
IDIOMS
成语